CONTENTS

CONTENTS

UNDERTAKER

HEIGHT: 6'10" **WEIGHT:** 299 lbs. **FROM:** Death Valley

SIGNATURE MOVES: Tombstone, Last Ride, Hell's Gate

DID YOU KNOW?: The most dominant Superstar of all time at *WrestleMania*, Undertaker has defeated 23 opponents at the "Show of Shows", including beating Kane, Triple H and Shawn Michaels more than once!

WWE Superstars come and go, but "The Deadman" is eternal. Even having his Streak broken at *WrestleMania 30* couldn't keep Undertaker down. He returned the next year at *WrestleMania 31* looking stronger and meaner than ever to defeat Bray Wyatt. After reclaiming his 'Mania dominance, Undertaker set his sights on Brock Lesnar and revenge, taking out "The Beast" with his Hell's Gate submission move. Now that Lesnar has awoken "The Deadman", nothing on Earth will save him!

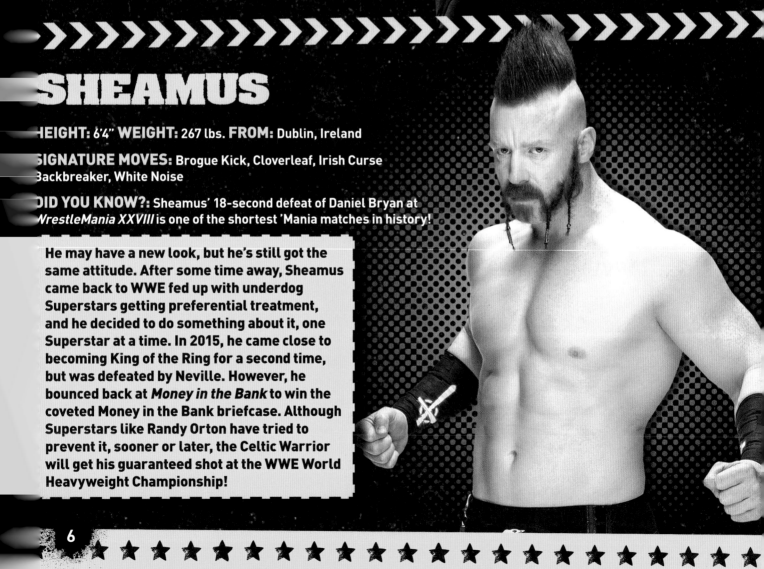

SHEAMUS

HEIGHT: 6'4" **WEIGHT:** 267 lbs. **FROM:** Dublin, Ireland

SIGNATURE MOVES: Brogue Kick, Cloverleaf, Irish Curse Backbreaker, White Noise

DID YOU KNOW?: Sheamus' 18-second defeat of Daniel Bryan at *WrestleMania XXVIII* is one of the shortest 'Mania matches in history!

He may have a new look, but he's still got the same attitude. After some time away, Sheamus came back to WWE fed up with underdog Superstars getting preferential treatment, and he decided to do something about it, one Superstar at a time. In 2015, he came close to becoming King of the Ring for a second time, but was defeated by Neville. However, he bounced back at *Money in the Bank* to win the coveted Money in the Bank briefcase. Although Superstars like Randy Orton have tried to prevent it, sooner or later, the Celtic Warrior will get his guaranteed shot at the WWE World Heavyweight Championship!

BROCK LESNAR

HEIGHT: 6'3" **WEIGHT:** 286 lbs.
FROM: Minneapolis, Minn.

SIGNATUARE MOVES:
F-5, Kimura Lock

DID YOU KNOW?: In only his second match at "The Showcase of the Immortals" in 10 years, Brock Lesnar shocked the WWE Universe by defeating Undertaker and breaking his 21-match *WrestleMania* winning streak!

Brock Lesnar was born and bred for only one thing: total destruction! As his advocate, Paul Heyman, says, a typical day for Brock follows a simple plan: Eat, Sleep, Conquer, Repeat. Lesnar is a competitor who never shows any weakness or mercy on his opponents, and anyone who stands in his way has bought themself a one-way ticket to Suplex City!

DEAN AMBROSE

HEIGHT: 6'4" **WEIGHT:** 225 lbs.
FROM: Cincinnati, Ohio

SIGNATURE MOVE:
Dirty Deeds

DID YOU KNOW?: Dean Ambrose held the United States Champions for 351 days, one of the longest WWE United States Championship reig in history.

Dean Ambrose is a ticking time bomb, and anyone who goes up against him is just lighting the fuse. As a former member of The Shield, he was always the wild card, ready to go off at a moment's notice. After surviving a battle with Brock Lesnar, starting his own talk show and his own match (both the Ambrose Asylum) there's nothing predictable to expect from The Lunatic Fringe.

FAMILY CONNECTIONS

IN WWE, TALENT SOMETIMES GOES BACK GENERATIONS. WE'VE GATHERED TOGETHER SOME FAMOUS SPORTS ENTERTAINMENT DYNASTIES. CAN YOU COMPLETE THESE FAMILY LINES FROM THE SUPERSTARS AT THE BOTTOM OF THE PAGE?

STARDUST

>>>>

Goldust

>>>>

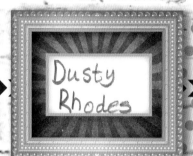
Dusty Rhodes

>>>>

ROMAN REIGNS

>>>>

Usos

>>>>

Rikish

>>>>

NATALYA

>>>>

Tysonkidd

>>>>

Bret Hart

>>>>

TRIPLE H

>>>>

Steaphine Mcmahon

>>>>

Vince McMahon

>>>>

8

SUPERSTAR *Scribble*

WE SPENT A DAY BACKSTAGE AT *RAW* GATHERING THESE AUTOGRAPHS, BUT NOW WE'RE NOT SURE WHO IS WHO! FROM THE LIST BELOW, CAN YOU MATCH EACH SIGNATURE TO EACH SUPERSTAR?

1

Seth Rollins

2

Brock Lesnar

3

Dolph Ziggler

4

Rusev

5

Stardust

6

Chris Jericho

7

Paige

8

Kevin Owens

9

Alberto Del Rio

AUTOGRAPHS

KEVIN OWENS   BROCK LESNAR   STARDUST

SETH ROLLINS   PAIGE   DOLPH ZIGGLER

CHRIS JERICHO   ALBERTO DEL RIO   RUSEV

ROYAL RUMBLE JUMBLE

SOMETHING CRAZY IS HAPPENING AT *ROYAL RUMBLE!* ALL THE SUPERSTARS AND THEIR SIGNATURE ITEMS HAVE SPILLED OUT OF THE RING!

EACH TIME YOU FIND SOMETHING FROM THE LIST BELOW HIDDEN IN THE JUMBLE, TICK IT OFF THIS LIST.

1. STARDUST'S STAR GLOVES ✓
2. BRAY WYATT'S LANTERN ✓
3. ALBERTO DEL RIO ✓
4. ERICK ROWAN'S SHEEP MASK ✓
5. MONEY IN THE BANK BRIEFCASE ✓
6. TRIPLE H'S SLEDGEHAMMER ✓
7. THE ASCENSION'S SHOULDER PADS ✓
8. SIN CARA'S MASK ✓
9. THE USOS ✓
10. PAIGE ✓
11. THE NEW DAY (EACH MEMBER) ✓
12. SETH ROLLINS ✓
13. JOHN CENA ✓
14. ROMAN REIGNS ✓

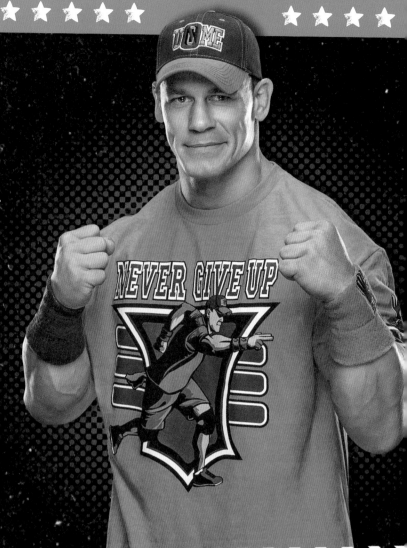

JOHN CENA

HEIGHT: 6'1" **WEIGHT:** 251 lbs.

FROM: West Newbury, Mass.

SIGNATURE MOVES: Attitude Adjustment, STF

DID YOU KNOW?: John Cena has won more titles at *WrestleMania* than any other Superstar.

More than a decade since his WWE debut, John Cena is stronger than ever! He won the United States Championship twice in 2015, most recently taking the title back from Seth Rollins. Always a fighting champion, Cena never shied away from defending his title, issuing an open challenge on a weekly basis. Still motivated by hustle, loyalty and respect, Cena is a 15-time World Champion, just one shy of the all-time record held by Ric Flair.

KEVIN OWENS

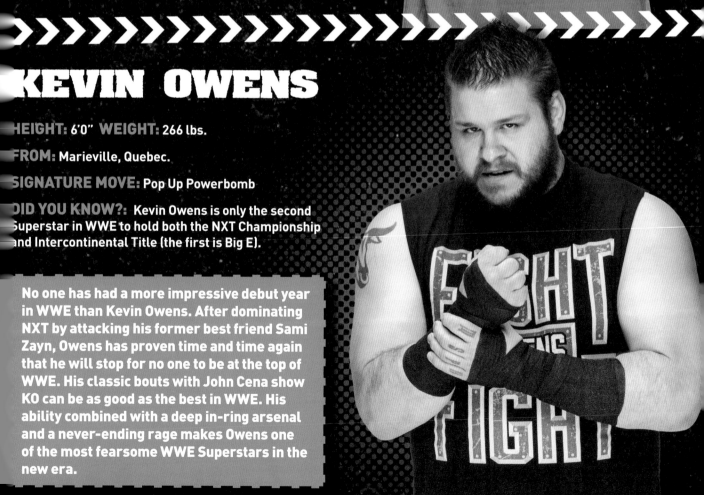

HEIGHT: 6'0" **WEIGHT:** 266 lbs.

FROM: Marieville, Quebec.

SIGNATURE MOVE: Pop Up Powerbomb

DID YOU KNOW?: Kevin Owens is only the second Superstar in WWE to hold both the NXT Championship and Intercontinental Title (the first is Big E).

No one has had a more impressive debut year in WWE than Kevin Owens. After dominating NXT by attacking his former best friend Sami Zayn, Owens has proven time and time again that he will stop for no one to be at the top of WWE. His classic bouts with John Cena show KO can be as good as the best in WWE. His ability combined with a deep in-ring arsenal and a never-ending rage makes Owens one of the most fearsome WWE Superstars in the new era.

ROMAN REIGNS

HEIGHT: 6'3" **WEIGHT:** 265 lbs.

FROM: Pensacola, Fla.

SIGNATURE MOVE: Spear

DID YOU KNOW?: In his first singles match at *WrestleMania*, Roman Reigns actually main-evented the show, facing Brock Lesnar for the WWE World Heavyweight Championship.

Although The Shield has broken up, Roman Reigns hasn't slowed down, even for a second! After winning the *Royal Rumble* in 2015, he landed a prime spot in the Main Event of *WrestleMania 31*, facing Brock Lesnar for the WWE World Heavyweight Championship! Although Reigns put up an incredible fight, he was undone by Seth Rollins, who cashed in his Money in the Bank contract and walked out with the gold! Since then, Roman has continued the fight, even teaming up with his former Shield-mate, Dean Ambrose, to take on the Wyatt Family at *SummerSlam*!

SETH ROLLINS

HEIGHT: 6'1" **WEIGHT:** 217 lbs.

FROM: Davenport, Iowa

SIGNATURE MOVE: Pedigree

DID YOU KNOW?: By cashing in his Money in the Bank contract at *WrestleMania 31*, Seth became the first Superstar to do so at the "Showcase of the Immortals".

Seth Rollins is a WWE Superstar who always knows how to make the most of an opportunity! After losing to Randy Orton at *WrestleMania 31*, Seth bounced back the same night and ran in on the Main Event to cash in his Money in the Bank contract. Just like that, the singles match became a Triple Threat, and one pinfall later, Seth was the new WWE World Heavyweight Champion! Later that year, he defeated John Cena to become both WWE World Heavyweight and United States Champion at once. Like him or not, Seth Rollins might be right when he calls himself the "Undisputed Future" of WWE.

JOHN CENA QUIZ

Think you have what it takes to be a member of Cenation? **Test your knowledge of all things Cena and see if you can become the Champ!**

1. Which famous TV star hosted *SummerSlam* and received an AA from Cena on *Raw*?

A. David Letterman
B. Jimmy Fallon
C. Steve Backshall
D. Jon Stewart ✓

2. What caused John Cena to lose the Cage Match against Bray Wyatt at 2014's *Extreme Rules* special event?

A. He saw a ghost
B. Erick Rowan made him disappear
C. A little boy sang "He's Got the Whole World in His Hands" ✓
D. Bray Wyatt hit him with the Sister Abigail

3. What was the name of John Cena's 2005 album?

A. Word Life
B. Basic Thuganomics ✓
C. You Can't See Me
D. The Champ is Here

4. Who did John Cena face in an open challenge in his WWE debut?

A. Batista
B. Kurt Angle ✓
C. Ric Flair
D. Triple H

5. Who did John Cena eliminate to win the 2008 *Royal Rumble*?

A. Edge
B. Mark Henry
C. Kane
D. Triple H ✓

6. TRUE OR FALSE John Cena has held the WWE Championship more times than any other Superstar?

False

7. With which two Superstars did Cena hold the tag team titles?

A. Zack Ryder and Daniel Bryan
B. Batista and Shawn Michaels ✓
C. Edge and Kofi Kingston
D. Dolph Ziggler and Randy Orton

8. John Cena has 15 World Championships. Which Superstar is he almost tied with?

A. Triple H
B. Bruno Sammartino ✓
C. The Rock
D. Ric Flair

9. Who did John Cena defeat to win his first World Championship?

A. Triple H
B. JBL ✓
C. Batista
D. Edge

10. Which NXT Superstar faced John Cena in a "Champion vs. Champion" match at *Elimination Chamber* in 2015?

A. Aiden English
B. Bull Dempsey
C. Kevin Owens ✓
D. Finn Bálor

11. As of *WrestleMania 32*, how many WrestleManias has John Cena main-evented?

A. 10 ✓
B. 5
C. 11
D. 3

12. **TRUE OR FALSE** John Cena was the first person to unsuccessfully cash in his *Money in the Bank* contract.

False

13. In college, John Cena played American football for his school's team? What position did he play?

A. Center
B. Tailback
C. Quarterback ✓
D. Linebacker

14. Where is John Cena from?

A. Stamford, CT
B. West Newbury, MA ✓
C. Dallas, Texas
D. New York City, NY

>>>>>>>>>>>>>>>>>>>>>>

15. How many brothers does John Cena have?

A. 4
B. 5
C. 3 ✓
D. 6

16. What was the first championship John Cena won in WWE?

A. Intercontinental
B. Tag Team
C. Cruiserweight ✓
D. United States

17. Who did John Cena defeat to become WWE Champion for a record-breaking ninth time?

A. Rey Mysterio ✓
B. The Rock
C. Bray Wyatt
D. Mark Henry

18. Which of these stipulation matches has John Cena not competed in?

A. Stretcher match
B. Ambulance match
C. Punjabi Prison ✓
D. "I Quit" match

19. Who attacked John Cena the night after his loss to The Rock at *WrestleMania XXVIII*?

A. Triple H
B. Batista
C. Randy Orton ✓
D. Brock Lesnar

20. Which Superstar helped Team Cena land the win at the 2014 *Survivor Series?*

A. Million Dollar Man
B. Sting ✓
C. Stone Cold Steve Austin
D. The Rock

21. Who did John Cena defeat at *WrestleMania 31* to become United States Champion?

A. Rusev ✓
B. Bray Wyatt
C. Seth Rollins
D. Big Show

Check your answers on page 76

HUSTLE ★ LOYALTY ★ RESPECT
JOHN CENA

CROSS WORDS!

Think you know your WWE Superstar catchphrases? We've assembled some of the best of all time here in this crossword puzzle! Use the word bank to help you!

ACROSS

1. "The ___Champ___ is here!"

3. Sin Cara and Kalisto say this twice: ___Lucha___

5. "Woo Woo Woo! You ___Know___ it!"

6. "Follow the _____!"

13. "I'm the Miz and I'm _____"

15. "When we say ____ y'all say 'O'!"

16. "I'm the _____ there is, the best there was and the best there ever will be!"

17. "___ the people!"

DOWN

2. "_____ of Dollars!"

4. "Viva La_____"

6. "And that's the _____ _____. Because Stone Cold said so!"

7. "Rest in _____!"

10. "D-Von, get the _____!"

11. "To be the man, you gotta _____ the man!"

12. "Eat, sleep _____ repeat!"

14. "You can't ___ me!"

WORD BANK

MILLIONS WE RAZA BEST LUCHA
UCE PEACE AWESOME TABLES SMELL
BEAT QUESTIONS CONQUER BUZZARDS
CHAMP SEE KNOW BOTTOM LINE

8. "Just when you think you know the answers, I change the _____!"

9. "If you _____ what The Rock is cooking!"

WE HAVE ONE MORE CHALLENGE FOR YOU...

WRITE DOWN ALL OF THE LETTERS IN THE YELLOW SQUARES, UNJUMBLE THEM AND FIGURE OUT WHICH SUPERSTAR IT SPELLS

The Rock

Crossword answers:
1. champ
2. (down) million
3. lucha
4. (down) raza
5. (down) know / known
6. buzzards
7. (down) peace / reaction
8. questions
9. smell
10. (down) tables
11. (down) beat
12. (down) conquer
13. awesome
14. (down) see
15. uce
16. best
17. we

17

MAZE MANIA

YOUR PATH TO GREATNESS BEGINS NOW! >>>>>>>>>>>>>>>>>>>>>>>>>>>>>>>>>>>>>>>

START
HERE
∨

WWE
NIGHT OF
CHAMPIONS

HELL IN A CELL

MONEY
IN THE
BANK

WWE
TLC
TABLES | LADDERS | CHAIRS

BATTLEGROUND

Every WWE Superstar dreams of making it all the way to *WrestleMania*, but getting there isn't easy! Can you make the journey all the way to the "Show of Shows", making sure you hit every pay-per-view along the way?

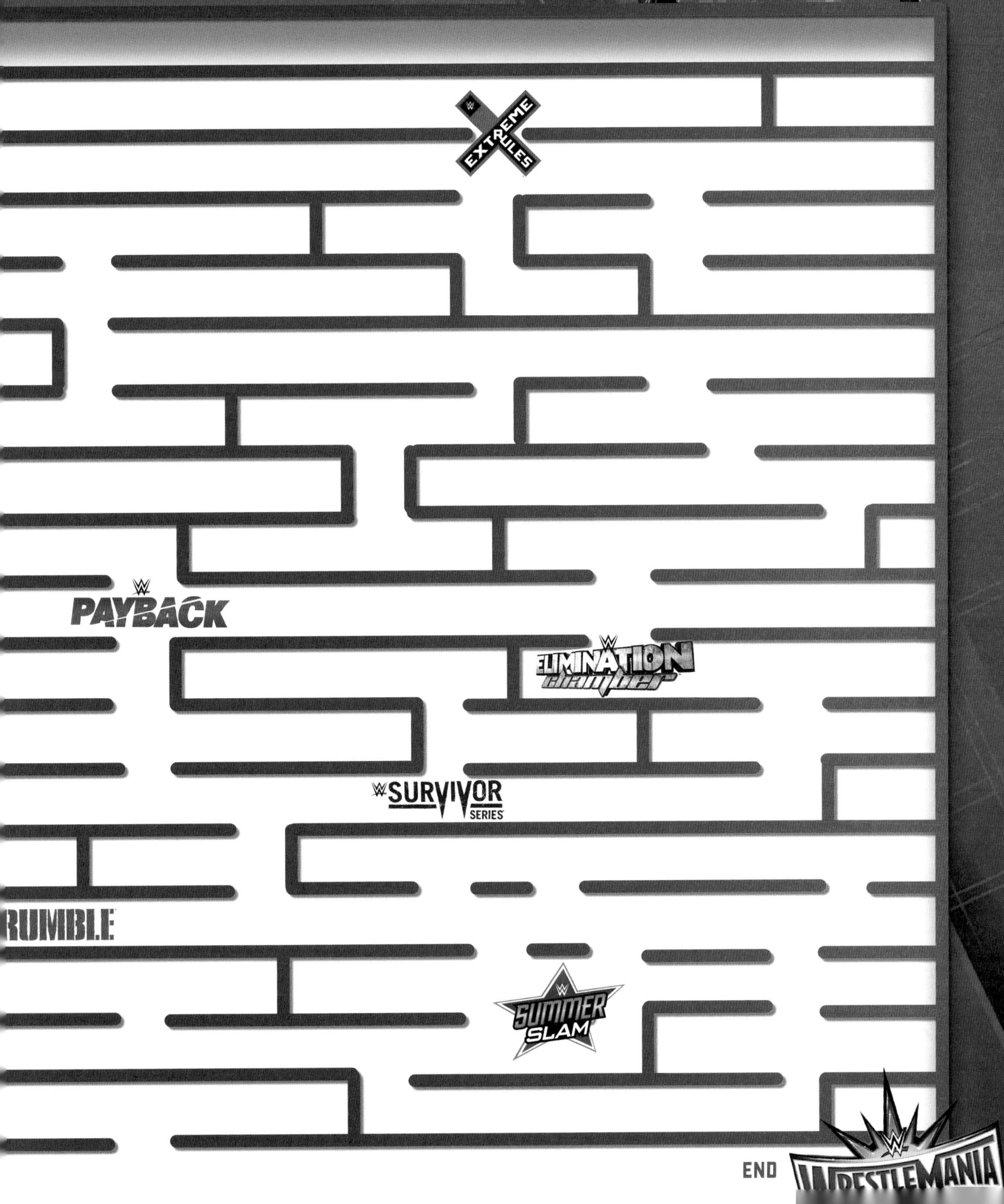

EXTREME RULES

PAYBACK

ELIMINATION chamber

SURVIVOR SERIES

RUMBLE

SUMMER SLAM

END WRESTLEMANIA

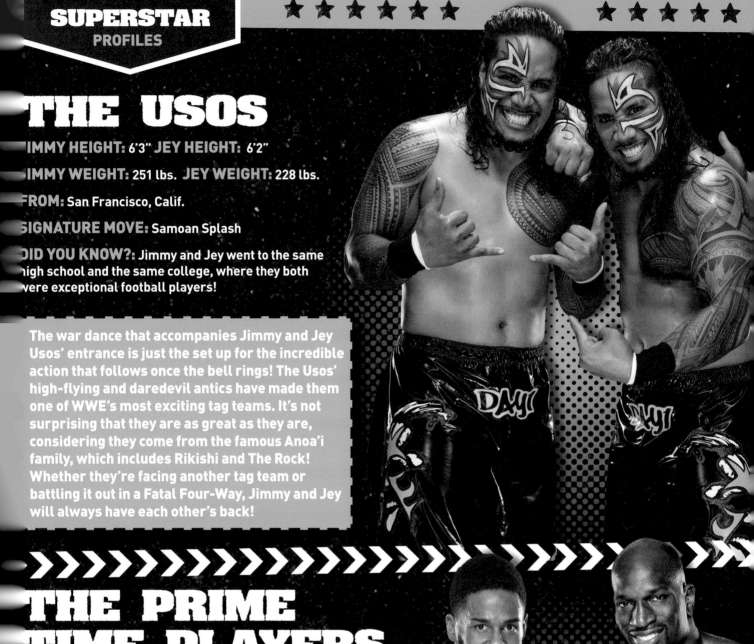

THE USOS

JIMMY HEIGHT: 6'3" **JEY HEIGHT:** 6'2"

JIMMY WEIGHT: 251 lbs. **JEY WEIGHT:** 228 lbs.

FROM: San Francisco, Calif.

SIGNATURE MOVE: Samoan Splash

DID YOU KNOW?: Jimmy and Jey went to the same high school and the same college, where they both were exceptional football players!

The war dance that accompanies Jimmy and Jey Usos' entrance is just the set up for the incredible action that follows once the bell rings! The Usos' high-flying and daredevil antics have made them one of WWE's most exciting tag teams. It's not surprising that they are as great as they are, considering they come from the famous Anoa'i family, which includes Rikishi and The Rock! Whether they're facing another tag team or battling it out in a Fatal Four-Way, Jimmy and Jey will always have each other's back!

THE PRIME TIME PLAYERS

DARREN YOUNG HEIGHT: 6'1"
TITUS O'NEIL HEIGHT: 6'6"

DARREN YOUNG WEIGHT: 239 lbs.
TITUS O'NEIL WEIGHT: 270 lbs.

DARREN YOUNG FROM: Miami, Fla.
TITUS O'NEIL FROM: Live Oak, Fla.

DARREN YOUNG SIGNATURE MOVE: Gut Check
TITUS O'NEIL SIGNATURE MOVE: Clash of the Titus

DID YOU KNOW?: Before becoming a WWE Superstar, Titus O'Neil was an arena football player for four years!

After a bitter break-up in 2014, the PTP came roaring back in 2015, reuniting and becoming stronger than ever! Although they impressed during their brief run as singles stars, "Mr. No Days Off" Darren Young and "The Real Deal" Titus O'Neil have proven to the WWE Universe that together they are an unbeatable force. At *Money in the Bank*, Titus and Darren shocked the world when they defeated The New Day to take home their first tag team titles! Whatever the future holds for The Prime Time Players, you can bet that it holds "millions of dollars!"

THE NEW DAY

KOFI HEIGHT: 6'0" BIG E HEIGHT: 5'11" XAVIER HEIGHT: 5'11"

KOFI WEIGHT: 212 lbs. BIG E WEIGHT: 204 lbs. XAVIER WEIGHT: 205 lbs

KOFI FROM: Ghana, West Africa BIG E FROM: Tampa, FL
XAVIER FROM: Atlanta, GA

KOFI SIGNATURE MOVE: Trouble in Paradise
BIG E SIGNATURE MOVE: The Big Ending
XAVIER SIGNATURE MOVE: Honor Roll

DID YOU KNOW?: New Day defend the tag team titles under the "Freebird Rule," meaning all three Superstars are considered champion!

The New Day are all about entertainment! Whether it's their lively entrance or their fast-paced manoeuvres in the ring, Xavier Woods, Kofi Kingston and Big E always deliver the best show possible. Relying on the power of positivity, The New Day are on a mission to keep the WWE Universe smiling, whether they want to or not! Of course, after *SummerSlam*, they were the ones who were smiling when they won back the tag team titles in a Fatal 4-Way match. Unfortunately, the next day they entered into a rivalry with the Dudley Boyz. But, no matter what opponent challenges them, nothing can break The New Day's spirits!

THE LUCHA DRAGONS

KALISTO HEIGHT: 5'6" SIN CARA HEIGHT: 5'7"

KALISTO WEIGHT: 170 lbs.

SIN CARA WEIGHT: 198 lbs.

FROM: Mexico City, Mexico

DID YOU KNOW?: The word "Lucha" means "fight" in Spanish!

Their signature chant of "Lucha! Lucha! Lucha!" is perfect for getting the WWE Universe fired up, but it's just a warm-up for the excitement that follows! Every time they step between the ropes, Kalisto and Sin Cara deliver fast-paced, gravity-defying action. They dazzled the crowd with their performance in the first-ever tag team Elimination Chamber Match at *Elimination Chamber*, and gave it their all in a Fatal 4-Way for the gold at *SummerSlam*. The Lucha Dragons are always ready to fight and take flight!

DESIGN A MASK

INSTRUCTIONS

1. Colour in the mask on the opposite page with any colours or style you want!

2. Cut out the mask along the dashed line with scissors. (If you don't want to cut out these pages in your Annual you could photocopy your mask)

   Ask a parent to help because scissors are sharp!

3. Make two holes in your mask to thread your elastic through and make a knot at each end to keep the elastic in place.

4. Devise a Superstar nickname and wear your mask with pride!

23

MONEY IN THE BANK MIX-UP!

SOME OF THE WWE SUPERSTARS TOOK IT UPON THEMSELVES TO DESIGN THEIR OWN MONEY IN THE BANK BRIEFCASES. BUT THEY'VE BEEN SWITCHED AROUND AND NO ONE KNOWS WHO OWNS THE PROPER CASE! CAN YOU HELP MATCH THE CASE TO THE SUPERSTAR BEFORE THEY LEAVE FOR THE NEXT TOWN.

"IF YOU WIN THIS CASE, YOU'LL STILL NEED THE COSMIC KEY TO OPEN IT!"

1. Stardust

"IF YOU WON THIS CASE, I BET YOU WOULD FIND PLENTY OF SWAG IN THIS BAG!"

2. Jack Swagger

"WIN THE CASE, AND GET THE TABLES!"

3. Dudleys

"GRABBING THIS CASE SHOULD BE EASY WHEN YOU'RE A HIGH-FLYER!"

4. Sin Cara

"THIS WAS A CASE DESIGNED FOR A MONSTER. CAREFUL YOU DON'T BURN YOURSELF WHEN YOU TOUCH IT!"

5. Kane

"IF YOU WON A CASE THIS AMAZING, YOU'D WANT TO SHOW IT OFF TOO!"

6. Dolph Zigler

"WANT TO GET YOUR HANDS ON THIS CASE? YOU'LL HAVE TO FORGET GRAVITY!"

7. Neville

"YOU NEED TO BE TWICE AS GOOD AS ANY OTHER SUPERSTAR IN ORDER TO COLLECT THIS CASE!"

8. Bellas

"BE THE ARCHITECT OF YOUR OWN FUTURE BY WINNING THIS CASE!"

9. Seth Rollins

"PEOPLE WILL BE TELLING YOU HOW MUCH YOU ROCK IF YOU WIN THIS CASE!"

10. New Day

"IF YOU CAN'T WIN THIS CASE ON YOUR OWN, PERHAPS YOUR FOLLOWERS, OR YOUR SISTER, CAN LEND A HAND!"

11. Bray Wyatt

"WINNING THIS CASE WILL DEFINITELY MAKE YOU SAY 'OOOOHHH!'"

12. Usos

"WIN THIS CASE AND YOU'LL BE WELL ON YOUR WAY TO STARTING YOUR OWN REVOLUTION!"

13. Paige

"EVEN IF YOU DIDN'T HOLD THE TITLE, PEOPLE WILL STILL CALL YOU CHAMP WITH THIS CASE!"

14.

★ ★ ★ ★ ★ ★ ★ ★ ★ ★ ★ ★

BECKY LYNCH

HEIGHT: 5'6"

FROM: Dublin, Ireland

DID YOU KNOW?: Becky Lynch was studying to be an actress before finding her career in sports entertainment.

With a world-class resume and a fiery personality to match, Becky Lynch is perhaps the most experienced newcomer to the Women's division. She wrestled all over the world and joined NXT looking to rise to the top of WWE. After a failed friendship with Charlotte and coming so close to winning the WWE Women's Title at *WrestleMania*, Lynch is looking to find the right grasp on the WWE mountain and become the first Irish born female grappler to wear the Women's Championship.

≫≫≫≫≫≫≫≫≫≫≫≫≫≫≫≫

CHARLOTTE

HEIGHT: 5'10"

FROM: Charlotte, NC

DID YOU KNOW?: Charlotte is the only women to win NXT Women's and WWE Women's Championships.

To say the world of sports entertainment is in Charlotte's genes is an understatement. Daughter of the two-time WWE Hall of Famer, Ric Flair, Charlotte has proven in her short time in WWE that she is a Flair through-and-through. Natural charisma, arrogance, confidence and not to mention her incredible athletic ability in the ring – it's no surprise she's leading the Women's Division movement in WWE today. If she's anything like her dad, we'll be seeing Charlotte for years to come inside a WWE ring.

★ ★ ★ ★ ★ ★ ★ ★ ★ ★ ★ ★ ★ ★ ★ ★ ★ ★ ★

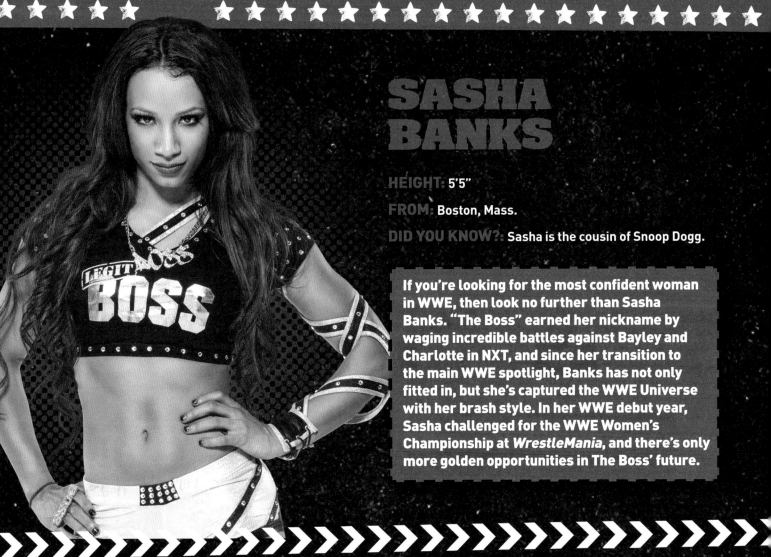

SASHA BANKS

HEIGHT: 5'5"

FROM: Boston, Mass.

DID YOU KNOW?: Sasha is the cousin of Snoop Dogg.

If you're looking for the most confident woman in WWE, then look no further than Sasha Banks. "The Boss" earned her nickname by waging incredible battles against Bayley and Charlotte in NXT, and since her transition to the main WWE spotlight, Banks has not only fitted in, but she's captured the WWE Universe with her brash style. In her WWE debut year, Sasha challenged for the WWE Women's Championship at *WrestleMania*, and there's only more golden opportunities in The Boss' future.

PAIGE

HEIGHT: 5'8"

FROM: Norwich, England

SIGNATURE MOVES:
Paige-Turner, Ram-Paige,
PTO (Paige Tapout)

DID YOU KNOW?: Paige is the first Superstar ever to hold both the NXT Women's Championship and the WWE Divas Championship.

Paige's WWE debut still ranks as one of the greatest of all time, but that was just the beginning! This British-born Superstar arrived on *Raw* the night after *WrestleMania 30* and won the Divas Championship in her very first match in WWE! Since then, she has been one of the most exciting and explosive competitors in WWE. Once part of Team PCB, Paige now stands alone, claiming that without her, there would be no Divas Revolution.

WHAT IS YOUR

★ ★ ★ ★ ★ ★ ★ ★ ★ ★ ★ ★ ★ ★ ★ ★

ARE YOU WILD?

HIGH-FLYER

ARE YOU A HIGH-FLYER?

YES

NO

ARE YOU A SOLO SUPERSTAR OR TEAM PLAYER?

SOLO

SUPERHEROES OR STAR WARS?

STAR WARS

TEAM

SUPERHEROES

DO YOU COME FROM A SMALL FAMILY OR LARGE FAMILY?

SMALL

DO YOU GET DIZZY?

YES

NO

LARGE

SAMOAN SPLASH

You're a free spirit with a lot of flash and style! You're not afraid to go up top and make a dive for the glory, but you like having a partner to watch your back as you sail through the air!

RED ARROW

You're part Superstar, part superhero, and gravity has nothing on you! You love to take to the skies, but you also love to give the WWE Universe a little bit of a show on the way back down to Earth!

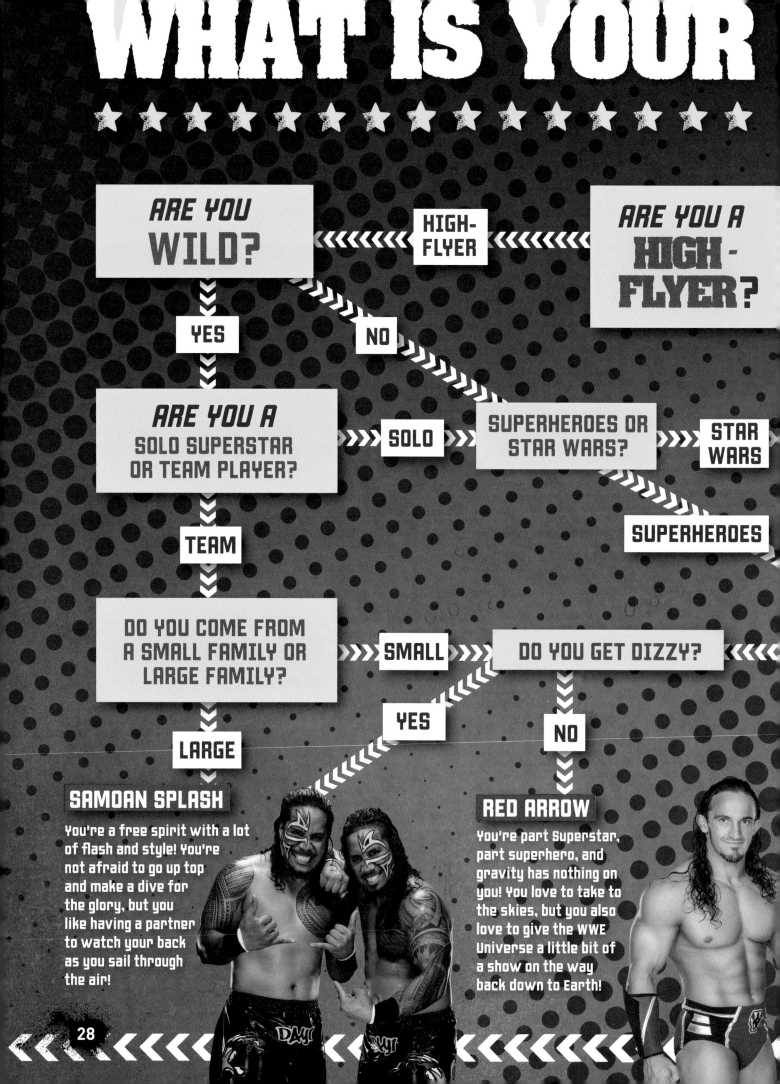

FINISHER?

You might have what it takes to step between the ropes, but what will you choose as your match-ending move? Answer these questions to find out what your opponents will be up against!

ARE YOU A MAT WARRIOR?

MAT WARRIOR →

RULE BREAKER OR RULE MAKER?

RULE BREAKER

RULE MAKER

EVER GOTTEN A FRIEND IN TROUBLE? → NO →

DO YOU HAVE A MOTTO?

YES

NO

YES

WOULD YOU WEAR A CAPE OUTSIDE OF HALLOWEEN?

YES

NO →

Would you ever side with the Authority?

YES

NO

PEDIGREE

A powerful, strong-willed battler, you like your finisher to make a statement. Keeping and honouring a legacy is important, but not nearly as important as taking out your opponents once and for all!

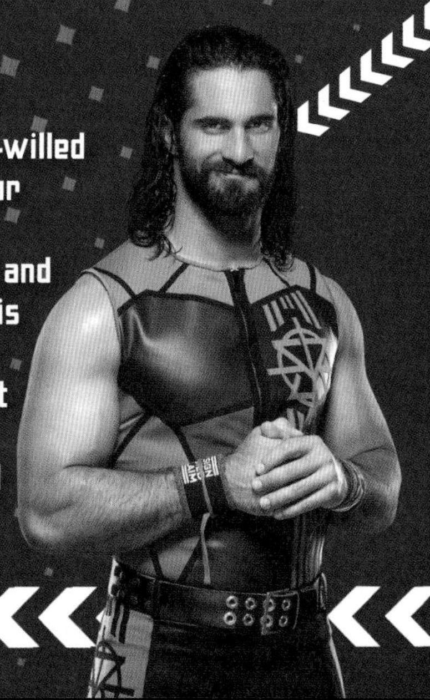

ATTITUDE ADJUSTMENT

When you put an opponent down, you make sure they stay down. You like your finisher to be a show of strength as much as a show of dominance. You rule the ring and you aren't afraid to let anyone know it!

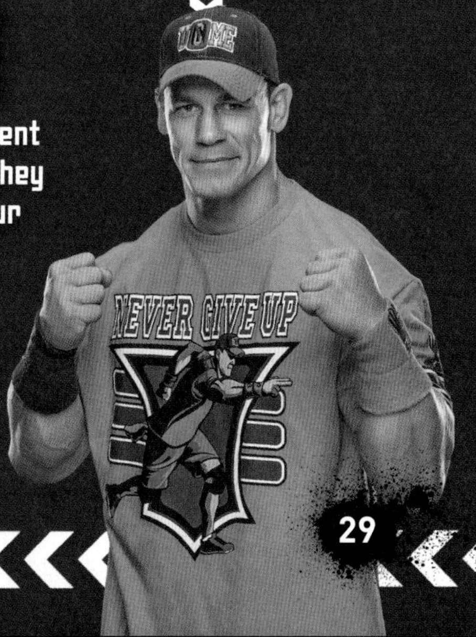

29

ROMAN REIGNS VS TRIPLE H

After Triple H eliminated Roman Reigns at the Royal Rumble and captured the WWE World Heavyweight Championship, the *WrestleMania* main event was set. Roman Reigns, the lone warrior would challenge the face of The Authority for ultimate WWE supremacy. The Game was ready, and Reigns was loaded. Which empire would rule WWE?

The Game and Stephanie McMahon made their entrance and vowed the WWE Universe would lose all hope, and ensured The Authority would continue to rule.

Roman Reigns entered AT&T stadium to a thunderous response and looked ready to compete in his second *WrestleMania* main event, and recapture his WWE World Heavyweight Title.

The Game, showing his years of ring experience, was quick to gain momentum and send Roman up and out of the ring early in the match with a clothesline.

Roman, however, turned the tide and started to play mind games against the Cerebral Assassin with a mock-DX salute to The Game.

Triple H wasted no time and went after Roman Reigns' reconstructed nose, which took Reigns out of action for weeks leading to *WrestleMania* with a series of punches to the face.

Reigns used his strength to take down Triple H with a series of clotheslines and delivered his signature Drive-By running dropkick to The Game on the ring apron.

With Stephanie McMahon distracting the ref, Triple H showed off his cerebral genius and delivered a low blow to the challenger. A dirty, but effective move.

As the action spilled outside the ring, Triple H went back to the nose, and drove Reigns' head into the German announce table. And delivered a swinging neck breaker from the table to the outside floor! Sprechen zie ouch!

In a rare sight, Triple H took to the skies and delivered a flying knee to Roman from the middle rope. The Game was pulling out all the stops. But after a second attempt, Roman was able to counter with an upper cut to face.

But that wasn't enough! Reigns, from out of nowhere, Speared The Game right through the barricade!

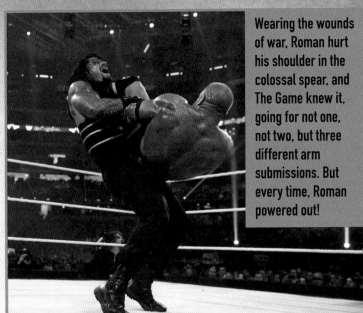

Wearing the wounds of war, Roman hurt his shoulder in the colossal spear, and The Game knew it, going for not one, not two, but three different arm submissions. But every time, Roman powered out!

SPEAR! This is it! Roman's going to win, but Stephanie distracts the ref and Triple H kicks out.

After the kick out, Stephanie entered the ring. . . .

And gets a Spear intended for Triple H!

Don't make The Game angry! Triple H delivers a Pedigree to Roman, but Reigns kicks out!

And Roman somehow gets the strength to deliver a Superman Punch!

Stephanie manages to hand Triple H his trademark sledgehammer.

But Reigns counters with another Superman Punch....

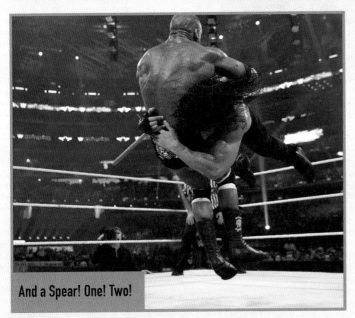

And a Spear! One! Two!

Three!

The renaissance of the "Roman Empire" finally begins! What's next for the new WWE World Heavyweight Champion?

UNDERTAKER VS SHANE MᶜMAHON

It was Legacy versus a *WrestleMania* career. Shane McMahon made a shocking return to WWE in early 2016 and went looking to take control away from his father. Vince McMahon then instantly pitted his son against Undertaker in Hell in a Cell for the power to run Monday Night Raw. But if The Deadman lost, it would have been his final *WrestleMania*. Undertaker was willing to destroy Shane for his *WrestleMania* legacy, but no one knew what Shane was willing to risk to change WWE.

Here Comes the Money! Shane McMahon makes his entrance with his sons, reminding the WWE Universe that this match is all about his legacy and the generations after him.

The Deadman arrives at *WrestleMania*. It's not *WrestleMania* without the aura of Undertaker.

Shane attempted to strike quickly and move away from Undertaker...

Delivering punches and even a spinning elbow...

But with Undertaker being the best pure striker in WWE, he stopped Shane and took the fight outside the ring.

Undertaker pulls out a signature move: his leg drop from the ring apron onto Shane. How much more can Shane O Mac take?

It doesn't take long for Undertaker to deliver his signature Last Ride to Shane. This is it, but no! Shane kicks out!

The steel steps are joining the fight and The Deadman introduces them to Shane with a Chokeslam. Shane, again, somehow manages to kick out.

Shane, getting a quick break with a seat on the steps, tells The Deadman to bring it.

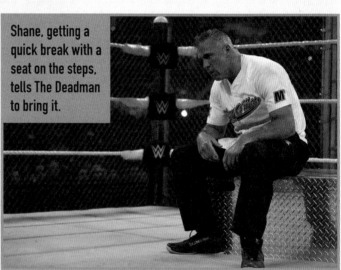

And drives Undertaker head first into the steel steps with a DDT.

But the momentum swings right back to Undertaker when he puts Shane in Hell's Gate!

After a few surprising blows, Shane set, and executed the Coast-to-Coast on Undertaker with a trash can to the face for added damage! But the Deadman took the blow and kicked out!

Shane, looking for another way to stop the Phenom, used bolt cutters to take down an entire portion and exit the Hell in a Cell.

But Undertaker barrelled Shane right through the cage wall!

Spring cleaning? Undertaker clears off the announce table...

And sends himself and Shane through one table after Shane attempted a sleeper! This match is awesome!

You know what might slow down a Deadman? A steel toolbox!

Shane's got that crazy look in his eyes.

Up Goes The Money! Now twenty-five feet in the air, at the top of the Hell in a Cell, Shane looks, measures and goes for everything!

And misses his moneymaking elbow drop!

Undertaker delivers the final nail in the coffin, and plants Shane with a Tombstone in the middle of the ring. One. Two. Three.

Undertaker will return to *WrestleMania*, but what does the future hold for Shane and his power over WWE?

LADDER MATCH FOR THE INTERCONTINENTAL TITLE

The idea is simple. Grab a ladder. Climb it. Grab the Intercontinental Championship hanging above the ring. Just be sure to avoid the other Superstars looking to do the exact same thing. This year, Dolph Ziggler, The Miz, Sami Zayn, Stardust, Sin Cara, Zack Ryder and Kevin Owens kicked off *WrestleMania* with a Seven-man Ladder Match for the Intercontinental Championship. But this match wasn't just for the gold; it was about creating a *WrestleMania* moment.

After all of the entrances, the seven Superstars face off in the ring all with the same purpose in mind.

While everyone attempts to get a ladder, Sami Zayn and Kevin Owens decide to trade fists at the start of the match.

The Miz is first to go for the gold, but Dolph Ziggler and Sami Zayn stop his efforts and The Miz takes a dive.

Former friends turned bitter rivals. Owens and Zayn square off again and KO back drops Zayn right onto a ladder!

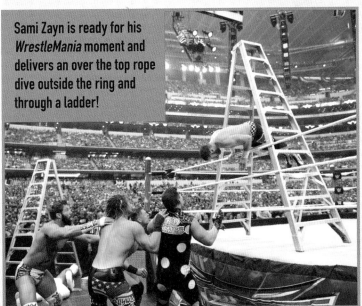

Sami Zayn is ready for his *WrestleMania* moment and delivers an over the top rope dive outside the ring and through a ladder!

Not to be outdone, Sin Cara blows everyone's mind by jumping off of a falling ladder to perform a springboard flip to the Superstars outside of the ring. *Lucha! Lucha! Lucha!*

Stardust, sensing an intergalactic force, pulls out his polka dot clad ladder, and looks to hit any Superstar who moves!

Zack Ryder delivers an El-Bro Drop from the top of the ladder to The Miz, who was just planted by Kevin Owens and a Pop-up Power Bomb! Couldn't happen to a nicer guy.

Owens throws Sin Cara off the ladder, onto Stardust and through a ladder! This match is awesome!

To ensure KO was out of the running, Sami annihilated Owens with a suplex onto a ladder. Oh! My! God!

After knocking down Sami Zayn, The Miz casually climbed up the ladder to grab the Title...

Only to get shoved off the ladder by Zack Ryder who captured his first ever Intercontinental Championship!

The new Champion celebrates in the ring with his father, and creates a classic *WrestleMania* moment.

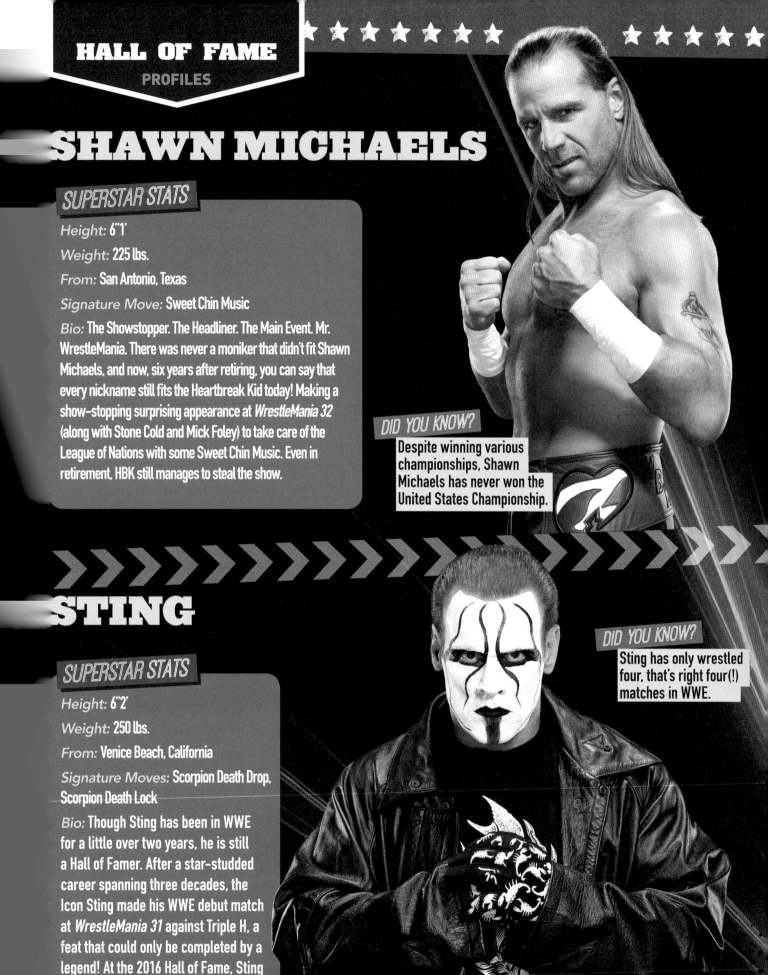

SHAWN MICHAELS

SUPERSTAR STATS

Height: 6"1'

Weight: 225 lbs.

From: San Antonio, Texas

Signature Move: Sweet Chin Music

Bio: The Showstopper. The Headliner. The Main Event. Mr. WrestleMania. There was never a moniker that didn't fit Shawn Michaels, and now, six years after retiring, you can say that every nickname still fits the Heartbreak Kid today! Making a show-stopping surprising appearance at *WrestleMania 32* (along with Stone Cold and Mick Foley) to take care of the League of Nations with some Sweet Chin Music. Even in retirement, HBK still manages to steal the show.

DID YOU KNOW?
Despite winning various championships, Shawn Michaels has never won the United States Championship.

STING

DID YOU KNOW?
Sting has only wrestled four, that's right four(!) matches in WWE.

SUPERSTAR STATS

Height: 6"2'

Weight: 250 lbs.

From: Venice Beach, California

Signature Moves: Scorpion Death Drop, Scorpion Death Lock

Bio: Though Sting has been in WWE for a little over two years, he is still a Hall of Famer. After a star-studded career spanning three decades, the Icon Sting made his WWE debut match at *WrestleMania 31* against Triple H, a feat that could only be completed by a legend! At the 2016 Hall of Fame, Sting announced his retirement, but promised it wouldn't be the last time the WWE Universe would ever see Sting.

RANDY "MACHO MAN" SAVAGE

SUPERSTAR STATS

Height: 6"2'

Weight: 237 lbs.

From: Sarasota, Florida

Signature Moves: **Top Rope Elbow Drop**

Bio: This Superstar inspired an entire generation of current and former WWE Superstars — it's safe to say that if it wasn't for Randy "Macho Man" Savage, there wouldn't be many Superstars today. The Macho Man captured the imaginations of the WWE Universe with his lavish costumes, intense demeanour, memorable mic skills and his incredible in-ring ability. Savage was the complete package and was able to transcend the ring and into mainstream culture, entertaining fans around the globe. Oooooh yeah!

DID YOU KNOW?

Savage was a second generation Superstar, son of wrestling legend, Angelo Poffo.

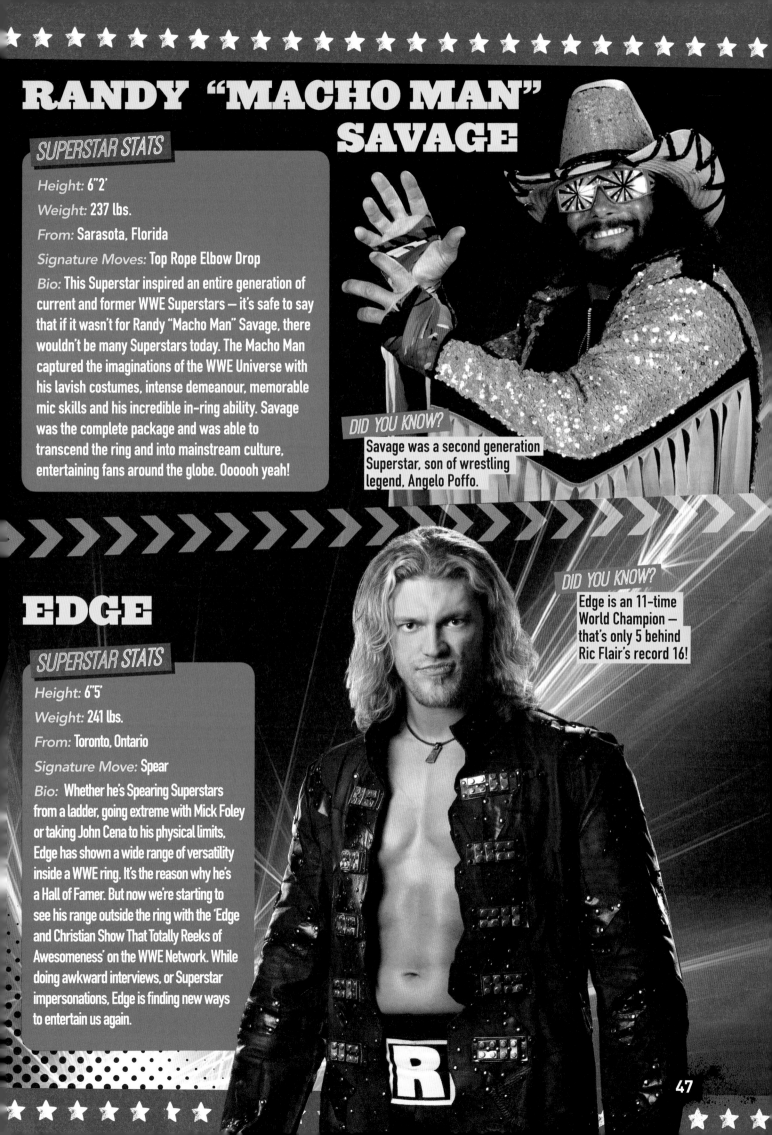

EDGE

DID YOU KNOW?

Edge is an 11-time World Champion — that's only 5 behind Ric Flair's record 16!

SUPERSTAR STATS

Height: 6"5'

Weight: 241 lbs.

From: Toronto, Ontario

Signature Move: **Spear**

Bio: Whether he's Spearing Superstars from a ladder, going extreme with Mick Foley or taking John Cena to his physical limits, Edge has shown a wide range of versatility inside a WWE ring. It's the reason why he's a Hall of Famer. But now we're starting to see his range outside the ring with the 'Edge and Christian Show That Totally Reeks of Awesomeness' on the WWE Network. While doing awkward interviews, or Superstar impersonations, Edge is finding new ways to entertain us again.

WWE BIG QUIZ

PART 1

Are you an expert of all things WWE? Try your hand at these tough questions and see if you're Superstar material!

QUESTION 01

WHAT WAS THE MAIN EVENT OF THE FIRST RAW OF 2016?

A	The New Day v The Usos	☐
B	John Cena v Alberto Del Rio	☐
C	Roman Reigns v Sheamus	✓
D	Roman Reigns v Kevin Owens	☐

QUESTION 02

WHAT WAS THE MATCH STIPULATION FOR THE MAIN EVENT OF *WRESTLEMANIA 30*?

A	Triple Threat	✓
B	Streak v Career	☐
C	No DQ	☐
D	Four-Way Elimination	☐

QUESTION 03

WHICH WWE HALL OF FAMER LIVED BY THE RULE-BREAKING CREDO OF, "LIE, CHEAT AND STEAL"?

A	Eddie Guerrero	✓
B	Eddie Graham	☐
C	Billy Graham	☐
D	Four-Way Elimination	☐

QUESTION 04

WHICH OF THESE SUPERSTARS WAS NOT KNOWN TO USE A SIGNATURE RULE-BREAKING OBJECT OF CHOICE?

A	Triple H	☐
B	Sting	☐
C	"Hacksaw" Jim Duggan	☐
D	Mr. Fuji	✓

QUESTION 05

WHICH OF THE FOLLOWING WILL NOT SCORE YOU A HELL IN A CELL VICTORY?

A	Pinfall	☐
B	Escaping the Cage	✓
C	Submission	☐

QUESTION 06

WHO HAS NEVER PARTNERED WITH CHRIS JERICHO TO WIN A TAG TEAM CHAMPIONSHIP?

A	Edge	☐
B	Christian	☐
C	The Rock	✓
D	The Miz	☐

QUESTION 07

HOW MANY TIMES HAVE THE USOS WON THE WWE WORLD TAG TEAM CHAMPIONSHIPS?

A	Zero	☐
B	One	☐
C	Two	✓
D	Three	☐

QUESTION 08

WHEN EDGE & CHRISTIAN WON THEIR THIRD TAG TEAM CHAMPIONSHIP THEY MASQUERADED AS A DISGUISED DUO NAMED...?

A	Los Luchadores	☐
B	Los Conquistadores	✓
C	Mr. Wrestling III & IV	☐
D	The Lucha Dragons	☐

QUESTION 09

WHICH THREE SUPERSTARS LOST THEIR WORLD CHAMPIONSHIPS TO A MONEY IN THE BANK WINNER FOLLOWING A CASHING-IN OF THE TITLE CONTRACT?

A The Miz, Batista, Christian ☐
B The Great Khali, Triple H, JBL ☐
C Shawn Michaels, Sheamus, Jack Swagger ✓
D John Cena, Undertaker, Chris Jericho ☐

QUESTION 10

WHICH SUPERSTAR HAS APPEARED IN THE MOST MONEY IN THE BANK LADDER MATCHES?

A Kane ☐
B Kofi Kingston ✓
C Christian ☐
D Dolph Ziggler ☐

QUESTION 11

WHICH OF THESE SUPERSTARS NEVER DEFEATED UNDERTAKER IN A ONE-ON-ONE HELL IN A CELL MATCH?

A Batista ☐
B Brock Lesnar ☐
C Shawn Michaels ✓
D Edge ☐

QUESTION 12

HOW MANY TIMES HAS RANDY ORTON BEEN CROWNED WORLD CHAMPION IN WWE?

A 8 ☐
B 12 ✓
C 9 ☐
D 11 ☐

QUESTION 13

WHICH OF THESE SUPERSTARS HAS NEVER WON THE *ROYAL RUMBLE*?

A Sheamus ☐
B Chris Jericho ✓
C Triple H ☐
D Mr. McMahon ☐

QUESTION 14

WHICH TEAM WAS ZACK RYDER NOT A PART OF?

A The Major Brothers ☐
B La Familia ✓
C The Hype Bros. ☐
D The Basham Bros. ☐

QUESTION 15

HOW MANY WEEKS DID WCW MONDAY NITRO DEFEAT WWE MONDAY NIGHT RAW IN THE RATINGS DURING THE MONDAY NIGHT WAR?

A 24 ☐
B 75 ✓
C 84 ☐
D 90 ☐

QUESTION 16

NEVILLE WAS ONCE THE LONGEST REIGNING NXT CHAMPION, BUT WHO DID HE DEFEAT TO WIN THE TITLE?

A Sami Zayn ☐
B Finn Balor ✓
C Bo Dallas ☐
D Samoa Joe ☐

QUESTION 17

WHAT CHAMPIONSHIP HAS RIC FLAIR NOT WON?

A European ✓
B U.S. ☐
C World Tag Team ☐
D Intercontinental ☐

QUESTION 18

KANE HAS WON TAG TEAM GOLD WITH WHICH SUPERSTAR?

A R-Truth ☐
B Mankind ✓
C Al Snow ☐
D Seth Rollins ☐

QUESTION 19

WE TOTALLY MADE UP A SUPERSTAR BELOW. SPOT THE FAKE.

A The Shockmaster ☐
B Gangrel ☐
C Phantasio ☐
D Bronx Honda ✓

QUESTION 20

WHO HAS NEVER WON A CHAMPIONSHIP IN WWE?

A Sting ☐
B Stephanie McMahon ✓
C Goldust ☐
D Kalisto ☐

Awesome Job! Check your answers on page 76!

W BIG QUIZ

PART 2

Can you spot out the fakes from the facts? Test your WWE knowledge and take the quiz to see if you're a WWE expert.

QUESTION 01

BROCK LESNAR IS A FORMER INTER-CONTINENTAL CHAMPION.

TRUE [ ] FALSE [✓]

QUESTION 02

BRAY WYATT IS UNDEFEATED IN HELL IN A CELL MATCHES.

TRUE [ ] FALSE [✓]

QUESTION 03

BATISTA HAS KICKED OUT OF THE UNDERTAKER'S TOMBSTONE!

TRUE [✓] FALSE [ ]

QUESTION 04

GOLDUST HAS NEVER BEEN IN A MONEY IN THE BANK MATCH.

TRUE [ ] FALSE [✓]

QUESTION 05

ROMAN REIGNS AND DEAN AMBROSE ARE FORMER TAG TEAM CHAMPIONS.

TRUE [ ] FALSE [✓]

QUESTION 06

THERE HAS NEVER BEEN A BRITISH BORN WWE CHAMPION.

TRUE [ ] FALSE [✓]

QUESTION 07

OHIO HAS NEVER HOSTED *WRESTLEMANIA.*

TRUE [✓] FALSE [ ]

QUESTION 08

CHRISTIAN WAS THE LAST EVER ECW CHAMPION.

TRUE [✓] FALSE [ ]

QUESTION 09
A CRYBABY MATCH IS A REAL MATCH IN WWE.

TRUE ✓   FALSE ☐

QUESTION 10
FANDANGO'S WWE DEBUT MATCH WAS AT SUMMERSLAM.

TRUE ☐   FALSE ✓

QUESTION 11
JOHN CENA HAS HAD A MATCH IN EVERY *WRESTLEMANIA* SINCE *WRESTLEMANIA* XX!

TRUE ✓   FALSE ☐

QUESTION 12
CESARO IS A SECOND-GENERATION SUPERSTAR.

TRUE ☐   FALSE ✓

QUESTION 13
PAIGE BECAME WWE DIVAS CHAMPION ON HER RAW DEBUT MATCH.

TRUE ✓   FALSE ☐

QUESTION 14
SUNDAY NIGHT HEAT WAS A WWE TELEVISION SERIES.

TRUE ✓   FALSE ☐

QUESTION 15
STING WAS A MEMBER OF THE FOUR HORSEMEN.

TRUE ☐   FALSE ✓

QUESTION 16
CHRIS JERICHO INVENTED THE MONEY IN THE BANK LADDER MATCH.

TRUE ✓   FALSE ☐

QUESTION 17
JBL WAS ONCE THE GENERAL MANAGER OF RAW.

TRUE ✓   FALSE ☐

QUESTION 18
MICK FOLEY PINNED CHRIS JERICHO DURING FOLEY'S HALL OF FAME SPEECH.

TRUE ✓   FALSE ☐

QUESTION 19
THE ROCK IS A FORMER UNITED STATES CHAMPION.

TRUE ✓   FALSE ☐

QUESTION 20
THERE WAS ONCE A WOMEN'S TAG TEAM CHAMPIONSHIP.

TRUE ✓   FALSE ☐

BIG QUIZ

PART 3

Can you figure out what's happening when the action is this close? Don't worry we added some hints.

Q1: NOT EVEN THE PRETTIEST SUPERSTARS ARE AS PRETTY AS ME?

Tyler Breeze

Q2: I'M THE NEWEST CHAMPIONSHIP IN WWE AND I DEBUTED AT WRESTLEMANIA 32.

Womens Championship

Q3: I'M AN OLD-FASHIONED TYPE OF VILLAIN.

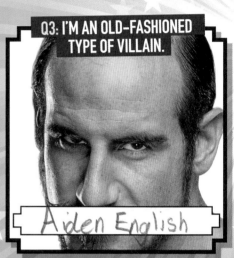

Aiden English

Q4: YOU CAN CONSIDER ME THE BOSS OF THE WWE'S WOMEN'S DIVISION.

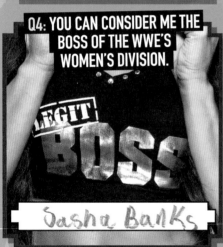

Sasha Banks

Q5: I LIKE TO TAKE MY COMPETITION OUT WITH A BIG SWING.

Cesaro

Q6: I FOLLOW THE BUZZARDS.

Luke Harper

Q7: GRAVITY HAS NO IDEA WHO I AM.

Neville

Q8: I ABSOLUTELY DO NOT LOOK STUPID.

Sheamus

Q9: I LOVE GIVING OUT HUGS! CONSIDER ME A HUGGER!

52

Q10: WHEN I'M OUT ON RAW, YOU CAN SAY THE MONEY IS ON THE WAY?

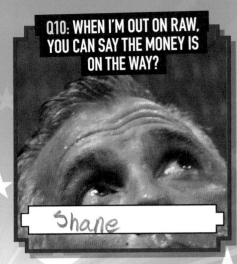

Shane

Q11: I'M A GUARANTEED SHOT AT THE WWE WORLD HEAVYWEIGHT CHAMPIONSHIP.

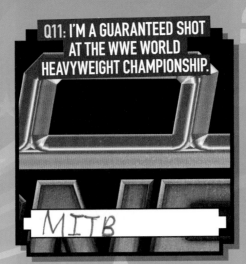

MITB

Q12: I CRUSH MY COMPETITION WITH MY BULGARIAN BRUTE STRENGTH.

Rusev

Q13: I'M A CERTIFIED G AND A BONA FIDE STUD. AND YOU CAN'T TEACH THAT.

Enzo Amore

Q14: IN MY LANGUAGE, I AM CONSIDERED FACELESS.

Sin Cara

Q15: WHEN YOU FIND OUT WHO I AM, YOU WILL THINK ALL RED EVERYTHING.

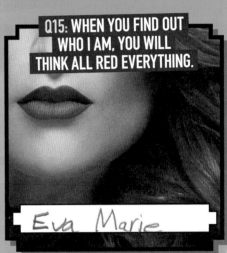

Eva Marie

Q16: I'M A SECOND-GENERATION SUPERSTAR WITH MORE HEART THAN THE REST.

Natalya

Q17: MY CLIENT WOULD BE VERY UPSET IF YOU DIDN'T KNOW MY NAME BY NOW.

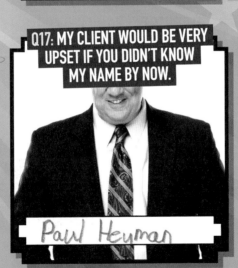

Paul Heyman

Q18: YOU DON'T WANT TO UNLEASH MY INNER DEMON!

Finn Balor

Q19: MY HIPS DON'T LIE AND MY TEAM TOTALLY ROCKS.

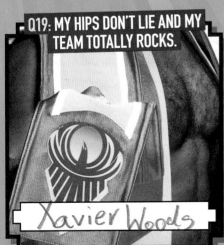

Xavier Woods

Q20: MY FRENCH-CANADIAN BEAUTY HAS NO EQUAL. AND MY AWESOME HUSBAND KNOWS THAT AS WELL.

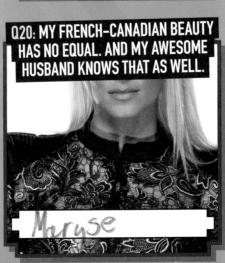

Maryse

Are you a **BIG** enough fan to know these answers?
Find out on page 76!

53

MIC DROP

The only thing as loud as a Superstars' moves is their trash talk. We listed 14 of the biggest boasters and their words of pain. Can you match the quotes to the correct grapplers?

QUOTE 01

In order to beat you, I have to have the match of my life. But having the match of my life is what I do!

WHO? AJ Styles

QUOTE 02

I am like death and taxes: inevitable!

WHO? Seth

QUOTE 03

I will prove you're not a machine, you're not a monster – you're a man with a pulse and you can be beat.

WHO?

QUOTE 04

You need to remember that I am the best in the world at what I do. Do you understand what I am saying to you, right now?

WHO? Jericho

QUOTE 05

Chris Jericho is going to stare at the guy who's going to turn Bon Jovi into Meatloaf!

WHO?

SETH ROLLINS   CESARO   ROMAN REIGNS   ENZO AMORE   NEW DAY   DOLPH ZIGGLER   PAIGE

QUOTE 06

Natalya is still a failure. Just like every woman in this division.

WHO?

QUOTE 07

I've never taken a hand-out and no one can take that away from me.

WHO?

QUOTE 08

They make sure you ain't booty!

WHO?

QUOTE 09

I got the gift of gab, and the gift of jab, and I'll put that lazy eye right back to work!

WHO?

QUOTE 10

This is my house!

WHO?

QUOTE 11

I wouldn't side with you, and I sure as hell wouldn't side with your egotistical, tyrannical, idiotic wife!

WHO?

QUOTE 12

Hey Miz! You're wearing your little thing – you're looking like a blind nun!

WHO?

QUOTE 13

The only movie you belong in is Jackass.

WHO?

QUOTE 14

My tongue is the sword of truth and it cuts through the deception of everything in your world.

WHO?

BRAY WYATT ★ AJ STYLES ★ SAMOA JOE ★ DEAN AMBROSE ★ CHARLOTTE ★ CHRIS JERICHO ★ THE ROCK ★

SPOT THE

WE CHANGED, REMOVED AND RE-EDITED 10 THINGS FROM THE PHOTOS BELOW. CAN YOU SPOT THE DIFFERENCES FROM PICTURE A TO PICTURE B? WE'LL EVEN SPOT ONE OUT FOR YOU TO GET YOU STARTED!

A

B

DIFFERENCE

THE ROAD TO WRESTLEMANIA

IT'S NEVER TOO EARLY TO START DREAMING UP THE BIGGEST BOUTS AT *WRESTLEMANIA*. AT THE TOP OF THE PAGE THERE ARE FOUR SUPERSTARS AND THEIR WINDING PATHS TO THE SHOW OF SHOWS AND THEIR POSSIBLE OPPONENTS. FOLLOW THE LINES TO FIND OUT OUR PREDICTIONS FOR A FUTURE *WRESTLEMANIA* SHAPE UP!

John Cena • Dean Ambrose • Bray Wyatt • Sami Zayn

Roman Reigns • Undertaker • The Rock • Kevin Owens

John Cena • Sami Zayn • Bray Wyatt • Dean Ambrose

got your unicorn horn, you have the New Day shirt, but
still feel like you're not an official member of the trio?
n't you dare be sour! Clap your hands and pick up a pencil and
aw yourself onto the front of Booty O's cereal box here and make
urself an official member. Because New! Day Rocks! New! Day Rocks!

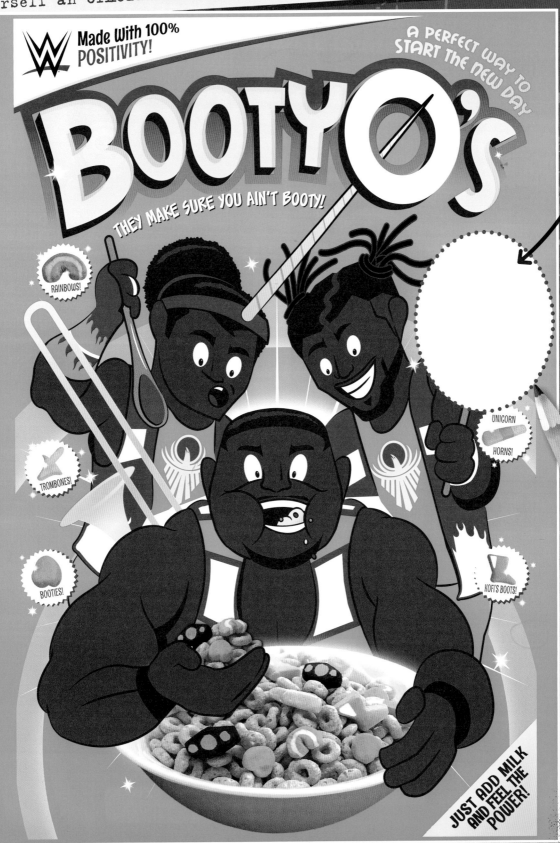

SUPERSTAR
SPIRIT ANIMALS

Every Superstar has a primal beast within them, which they channel to unleash their ring fury! Can you match these Superstar-soul-connected-spirit animals to their grappler?

1 HONEY BADGER

"I'm unstable, unpredictable and prefer madness over order. When a target's in my sights, there ain't no stopping me. I like a good fight, even when the odds are against me. But you should never count me out. You can say I should be committed to an asylum."

MY SUPERSTAR IS...
Dean Ambrose

2 BLACK PANTHER

"I'm not a bad cat. I'm not a good cat. I'm the cat! I bring the fight to my prey hard, and often, creating an empire of destruction behind me. I have Super-Cat speed and lunge like a Spear! No matter the odds, I can and I will survive. You can believe that."

MY SUPERSTAR IS...
Roman R

3 LION

"I am the king of the jungle, and the ruler of the land. I survey my territory with my killer instinct and cerebral genius. Thanks to my Pedigree, I will rule this kingdom for years and years. All hail the king."

MY SUPERSTAR IS...

Triple H

4 WOLF

"I'm a lone wolf. I walk alone and I don't like anyone. I'm the current king of battles, both royal and minor. And I'm only just getting started! If you come across my path, it will be the End of Days for you."

MY SUPERSTAR IS...
Baron Corbin

⑤ VIPER

"I strike quickly and suddenly. My attacks come out of nowhere! I have generations of snake lineage in my blood, making me the Apex Predator. When I strike, my prey is knocked out cold. Really Knocked Out."

MY SUPERSTAR IS...

⑥ BUZZARD

"I travel in a group of three or sometimes four other birds. I'm a bird, but I can also walk like a spider. I'm very comfortable around fireflies in the dark, and if I could, I would eat the world. You can always follow me."

MY SUPERSTAR IS...

⑦ BULL

"I'm known all over the world by millions...and millions of people. I can electrify like no other. And in a fight, I always bring it! If you cross my path, you will hit Rock Bottom. If I was a chef, you'd love the smell of my cooking."

MY SUPERSTAR IS...

⑧ ALIEN

"My synaptic stimulants have told me about the world beyond this galaxy, beyond the physical dimensions and the human mind! That's why I am the ruler of Dark Matter. And all of my prey fall to the Queen's Crossbow."

MY SUPERSTAR IS...

⑨ PEACOCK

"Flashy, loud and cocky, there's no denying I grab your attention and love my own reflection. I'm awesome, and I am must-see. The only A-lister in the animal kingdom, I will out class every animal on my looks alone."

MY SUPERSTAR IS...

Check out whether you're 'Top Dog' on page 77!

ROYAL KNOCKOUT

Who's going to main event WrestleMania?

2   3   4   5   6   7

GROUP A

GROUP B

HOW TO PLAY:

1. Each player chooses a group (A, B, C or D).
2. Start the game by rolling both dice, then add up the total.
3. Check which Superstar matches the number thrown.
4. If any player has that team in their group, cross them out.
5. Choose who will roll next and repeat step 1 to 4 as many times as it takes until a player has crossed out all the teams in their group. KNOCKOUT!
6. The first player to cross out all the teams in their group is the ROYAL RUMBLE WINNER!

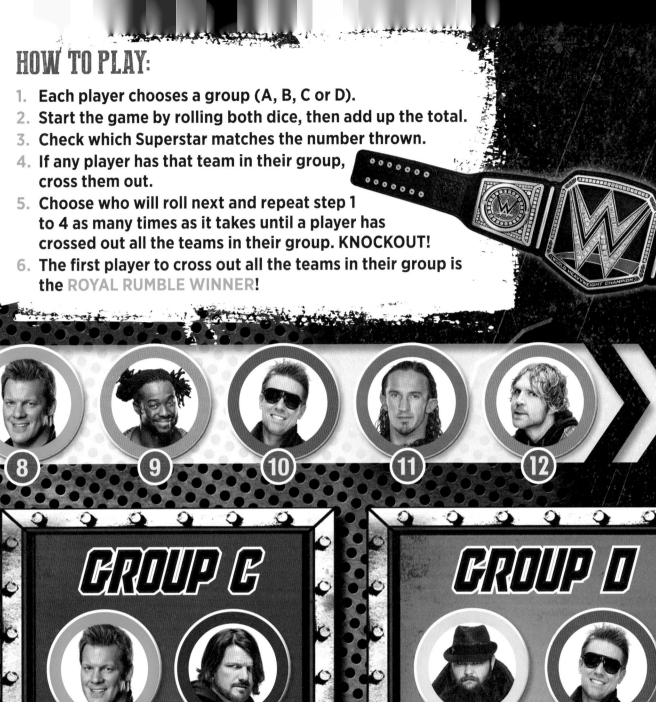

8   9   10   11   12

GROUP C

GROUP D

THIS WILL BE MY YEAR

Take note now, 2017 will be a HUGE year for these Superstars, and here's why!

BRAY WYATT

The Eater of Worlds has already shown the WWE Universe things they've never seen before, but in 2017 we will see only more intrigue and mystery from Wyatt. We speculate new opponents, new allies or perhaps even some new alliances, but it's hard to determine anything with Bray. One thing is for sure, Wyatt will surely continue to show us things we've never seen before.

ENZO & CASS

These two guys might already be the realest guys in the room, but sooner or later, they will alter the WWE Tag Team division like no team before them. We foresee the duo not only capturing gold, but also conquering the biggest teams in WWE.

SETH ROLLINS

Don't call it a comeback! We predict that Seth Rollins will stop at nothing to win back his WWE World Heavyweight Championship. But with the Championship picture changing so much since Rollin's injury side-lined him from the ring, he's going to have a lot of new, unforeseen contenders to deal with, but that's never stopped The Architect from a challenge before.

DEAN AMBROSE

It's hard to foresee someone as unstable as Dean Ambrose, but we know one thing for sure, there's nothing but success headed his way. With Dean taking on such legendary Superstars like Brock Lesnar and Chris Jericho in 2016, he's bound to take more bites out of the biggest Superstars in WWE. And you can't beat what you can't understand.

FUTURESTARS!

Can you accurately foretell the fortune of Superstars? Fill in the banks and check back in a year and see how well your crystal ball works.

THIS TIME NEXT YEAR, I THINK THE WWE WORLD HEAVYWEIGHT CHAMPION WILL BE.........

THIS TIME NEXT YEAR, I THINK THE WWE WOMEN'S CHAMPION WILL BE......

THIS TIME NEXT YEAR, I THINK SOMEONE IS GOING TO TURN BAD AND IT WILL BE......

THIS TIME NEXT YEAR, I THINK SOMEONE IS GOING TO TURN GOOD AND IT WILL BE.....

THIS TIME NEXT YEAR, I THINK UNDERTAKER WILL BATTLE ONCE AGAIN AT *WRESTLEMANIA*, BUT THIS TIME AGAINST......

SASHA BANKS

She's The Boss and quite possibly the most talented Superstar to come out of NXT in the Women's division. Sasha has all the confidence in the world to overcome any challenge, but can she finally conquer Charlotte to win her first WWE Women's Championship? Whether Charlotte is the Champ or not, she will surely be Sasha's biggest foe in her already impressive career.

AJ STYLES

He shocked the entire WWE Universe with his debut at the Royal Rumble in 2016, and considering Styles' resume, he has a lot more phenomenal left within him. With his Club buddies, Luke Gallows and Karl Anderson joining WWE, it's hard not seeing Styles and company overtaking and ruling WWE in 2017. And who knows, maybe we might see new members joining The Club.

KEVIN OWENS

We doubt his attitude will change, but KO is destined to make WWE history in 2017. His very short tenure in WWE has been extremely impressive and if he can defeat John Cena on his debut match, then what can he accomplish when he's at the right time and right place? We wouldn't be surprised if we're calling Owens WWE World Heavyweight Champ by this time next year.

THE NEW DAY

All good things must come to an end, and we hate to be sour, but we foresee the New Day dividing and conquering the WWE in an all-new way. Let's be clear, we don't think New Day will split, they will simply look to capture all the gold in the WWE, because what could be more positive than three best friends all holding their own championship?

BROCK LESNAR

Is it possible for Brock Lesnar to have a bad year? Probably not. After breaking the Streak and an impressive run as WWE World Heavyweight Champ, we predict Brock will alter the course of Suplex City and look for new types of challenges to conquer. Brock has never been in a Money in a Bank match, nor has he ever faced various new members of the WWE roster including Kevin Owens and Cesaro. We think Lesnar is in for an interesting 2017.

EVA MARIE

Our boldest prediction yet, but we see Eva Marie surprising and surpassing all expectations and making a major impact in the WWE Women's Division in and out of the ring. We see the Women's division running red with jealousy as Eva wins her first taste of gold in WWE in 2017.

NEXT YEAR WE'RE GOING TO SEE THE WWE HALL OF FAME GET A NEW MEMBER AND IT WILL BE.......

THIS TIME NEXT YEAR, I THINK WE'RE GOING TO HAVE A NEW PERSON RUNNING RAW AND IT WILL BE.........

THIS TIME NEXT YEAR, I THINK THIS TAG TEAM WILL SPLIT UP AND GO THEIR SEPARATE WAYS........

THIS TIME NEXT YEAR, I THINK WE'RE GOING TO HAVE A NEW TAG TEAM OF......

THIS TIME NEXT YEAR, I THINK THIS NXT SUPERSTAR WILL BE ON RAW OR SMACKDOWN........

HIGH FIVE

We ranked the top five biggest, baddest and best things all across WWE. Take five, and witness how awesome WWE can be in just 5 ways.

TOP 5 STRONGEST SUPERSTARS

1. John Cena
2. Cesaro
3. Brock Lesnar
4. Big E
5. Braun Strowman

TOP 5 MASKS

1. Kane
2. Kalisto
3. Sin Cara
4. Mankind
5. Eric Rowan

TOP 5 BEST FACE-PAINT DESIGNS

1. Finn Balor
2. Ultimate Warrior
3. The Usos
4. Stardust
5. Sting

TOP 5 SCARIEST SUPERSTARS

1. The Boogeyman
2. Kane
3. Papa Shango
4. Jake "The Snake" Roberts
5. Undertaker

TOP 5 TALLEST SUPERSTARS

1. Andre The Giant 7"4
2. Big Show, 7"0'
3. Kane, 7"0'
4. Undertaker 6"10'
5. Luke Gallows, Braun Strowman & Big Cass, tied at 6'8"

TOP 5 MOST CHAMPIONSHIP WINS

1. John Cena, 12 WWE World Heavyweight Championships
2. Edge, 14 World Tag Team Championships
3. Chris Jericho, 9 Intercontinental Championships
4. The Dudleys, 9 Tag Team Championships
5. John Cena, 5 United States Championships

TOP 5 COOLEST LEGENDS RING GEAR

1. Goldust
2. Legion of Doom
3. Randy "Macho Man" Savage
4. Ultimate Warrior
5. Ric Flair

TOP 5 SUPERSTARS WITH THE BEST TATTOOS

1. Undertaker
2. Randy Orton
3. The Rock
4. Brock Lesnar
5. Roman Reigns

TOP 5 WEIRDEST HAIRDOS

1. Sheamus
2. Rocky Maivia
3. Scotty 2 Hotty
4. Red Rooster
5. Tyson Kidd's original 'do

TOP 5 FASTEST SUPERSTARS

1. Neville
2. Kofi Kingston
3. Kalisto
4. AJ Styles
5. Sin Cara

RECORDS ARE

This year's *WrestleMania* absolutely shattered the all-time record attendance with 101,763 members of the WWE Universe filling AT&T Stadium. With that, we dug up the biggest records in WWE history and ponder what records will be broken in 2017.

454

Days the Honky Tonk Man held the Intercontinental Championship, the longest Intercontinental Championship reign in WWE history.

16

Matches during one *WrestleMania*. The honour goes to *WrestleMania IV*, where Randy "Macho Man" Savage won the night's final match (and his fourth) to earn the vacant WWE Championship in a one-night tournament.

24

The age of Randy Orton when he became the youngest World Heavyweight Champion in history, at SummerSlam 2004.

12

Eliminations made by Roman Reigns in the 2014 Royal Rumble – the most ever made by a single Superstar.

39

Speaking of the Royal Rumble, Shawn Michaels holds the record for most career Rumble eliminations, 39, spanning 20 years.

14

Tag Team Championships won by Edge, the most in WWE history. Edge has shared the gold with five different partners: Christian, Chris Jericho, Hulk Hogan, Randy Orton and Rey Mysterio.

MADE TO BE BROKEN

2,803
Days Bruno Sammartino held the WWE Championshi – that's almost eight years. The Hall of Famer is the longest reigning WWE Champion of all time.

14
Hell in a Cell is officially Undertaker's playground, owning the most appearances inside the steel and also the most victories with a record 7.

28
Years Fabulous Moolah held the Women's Championship, making her not only the longe reigning Women's Champ, but also the longest reigning champ in WWE history!

8
Elimination Chamber Matches competed in by Chris Jericho – more than any other Superstar. He also holds the record for most eliminations, ten, but most Chamber victories go to Triple H with four.

16
World Championsh held by Ric Flair through his illustri career – the most World Title victorie by any Superstar. However, John Cen is close to tying Fla longstanding recor with 15.

69:52

The running time of the longest Royal Rumble Match in 2011, when Alberto Del Rio won the first and only 40-man Royal Rumble Match

WWE GOES VIRAL

 CLICK HERE! Do you want to watch now? Scan the QR code with your smart phone to launch YouTube so you can watch these awesome videos right now!

MOST WATCHED MATCHES

There are a lot of full-length matches on YouTube, but these three rank in the millions (and millions) of views. These forgotten gems turned viral classics are all historic, momentous matches that shaped WWE for years to come.

41-Man Battle Royal on SmackDown
https://www.youtube.com/watch?v=n3PswaGlZt4

John Cena & Randy Orton vs. the entire Raw roster
https://www.youtube.com/watch?v=ndgVcE7w0uo

20-Man Battle Royal on SmackDown for World Heavyweight Championship
https://www.youtube.com/watch?v=bQnvyk6jRZc

TOP TEN

It's in the name! The Top 10 will list the greatest, unforgettable, funniest and brutal moments in WWE history. If you're looking for a list of the best, well look no further.

Referees Get Wrecked
https://www.youtube.com/watch?v=up9oc3A0OpI

Best Fan Reactions - WWE Top 10
https://www.youtube.com/watch?v=zwTRHfEMq7k

Slip and Slide
https://www.youtube.com/watch?v=NNGTYcB7kO4

Ring Wrecking Moments
https://www.youtube.com/watch?v=PNkpmEukXF4

Most Outrageous Superstar Pranks
https://www.youtube.com/watch?v=683hzaj3oc8

WWE GAME NIGHT

Join host Heath Slater in this fun game show where WWE Superstars participate in games that you play! From Dodgeball to Heads Up – who wins? You do!

WWE Pie Face
https://www.youtube.com/watch?v=m-CtrDuXehg

WWE Dodgeball
https://www.youtube.com/watch?v=OIllJVEFyYU

WWE Heads Up
https://www.youtube.com/watch?v=nGXsQOLG_KA

Superstar impersonation challenge
https://www.youtube.com/watch?v=FtPlHWa-MAc&index=4&list=PLqIVmFaHA8BqiUOH6jBBLkKDYrhff1zGy

FUNNY

There's a lot of funny moments in WWE history, good thing the video historians put the best clips together for your viewing pleasure. Get ready to start laughing.

WWE Superstars and Lasers
https://www.youtube.com/watch?v=qdA-a8-gw4M

Happy Holidays from WWE
https://www.youtube.com/watch?v=sa7fg6avugY

5 WWE Superstars as Kids: 5 Things
https://www.youtube.com/watch?v=YCNpQlu5M6c

WWE's Funniest Moments
https://www.youtube.com/watch?v=Oec3jC3sQwk

The New Day gives Michael Cole a job evaluation
https://www.youtube.com/watch?v=HlKXBV41LCw

ONE VERSUS ALL

ROMAN REIGNS

the legit BOSS

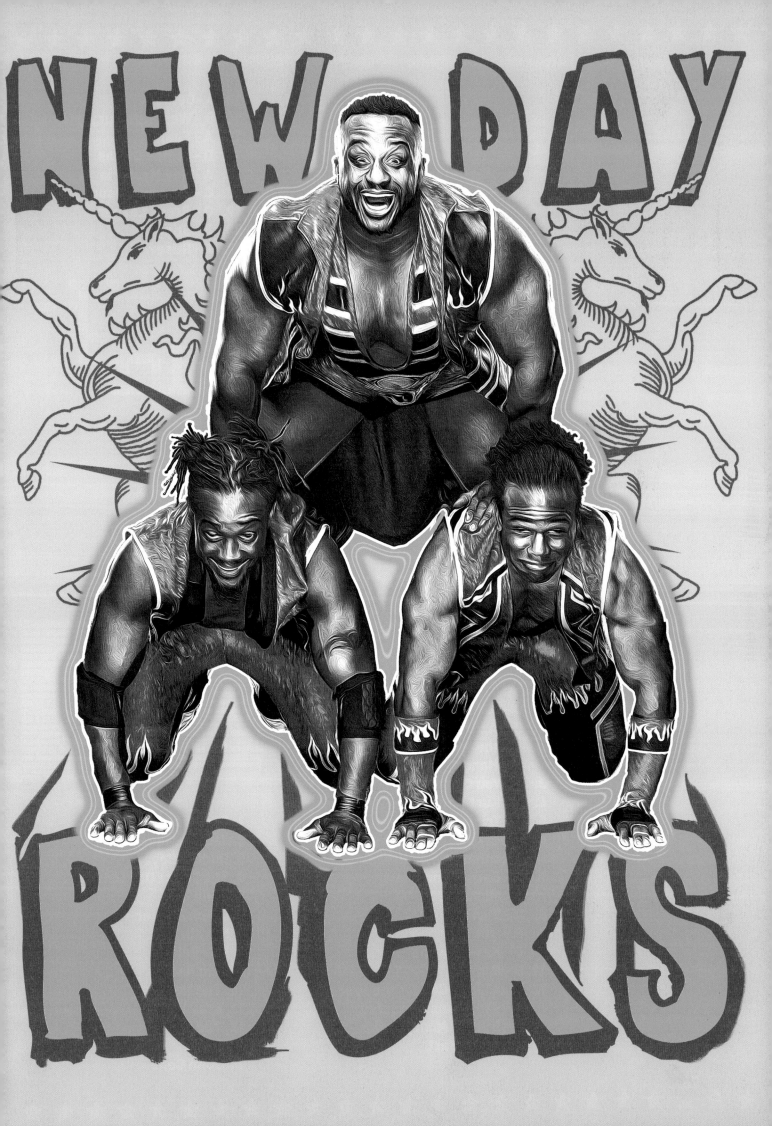

08 Family Connections

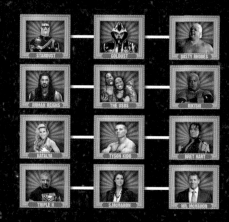

09 Superstar Scribble

1. Seth Rollins
2. Brock Lesnar
3. Dolph Ziggler
4. Rusev
5. Stardust
6. Chris Jericho
7. Paige
8. Kevin Owens
9. Alberto del Rio

10 *Royal Rumble* Jumble

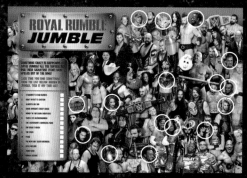

14 The Ultimate John Cena Quiz

1. D - Jon Stewart
2. C - A little boy sang "He's Got the Whole World in His Hands"
3. C - You Can't See Me
4. B - Kurt Angle
5. D - Triple H
6. True. As of press time, he has held that title 12 times.
7. B - Batista and Shawn Michaels
8. D - Ric Flair
9. B - JBL
10. C - Kevin Owens
11. B - 5
12. True. John Cena is the first person to unsuccessfully cash in his *Money in the Bank* contract.

13. A - Center
14. B - West Newbury, MA
15. A - Four
16. D - United States
17. A - Rey Mysterio
18. C - Punjabi Prison
19. D - Brock Lesnar
20. B - Sting
21. A - Rusev

16 Cross Words!

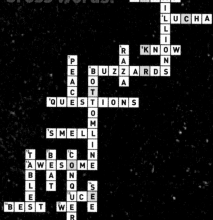

EXTRA CHALLENGE
THE UNJUMBLED LETTERS SPELL
THE ROCK

18 Maze Mania

24 Money In The Bank Mix-up

1. Stardust
2. Jack Swagger
3. Dudley Boyz
4. The Lucha Dragons
5. Kane
6. Dolph Ziggler
7. Neville
8. The Bellas
9. Seth Rollins
10. The New Day
11. Bray Wyatt
12. The Usos
13. Paige
14. John Cena

48 Big Quiz Part 1

1. C	11. D
2. A	12. B
3. A	13. B
4. D	14. D
5. B	15. C
6. D	16. C
7. C	17. A
8. B	18. B
9. D	19. D
10. A	20. A

50 Big Quiz Part 2

1. FALSE	11. FALSE
2. FALSE	12. FALSE
3. TRUE	13. TRUE
4. TRUE	14. TRUE
5. FALSE	15. TRUE
6. TRUE	16. TRUE
7. TRUE	17. FALSE
8. FALSE	18. TRUE
9. TRUE	19. FALSE
10. FALSE	20. TRUE

52 Big Quiz Part 3

1. Tyler Breeze
2. WWE Women's Championship
3. Aiden English
4. Sasha Banks
5. Cesaro
6. Luke Harper
7. Neville
8. Sheamus
9. Bayley
10. Shane McMahon
11. Money In The Bank Briefcase
12. Rusev
13. Enzo Amore
14. Sin Cara
15. Eva Marie
16. Natalya
17. Paul Heyman
18. Finn Balor
19. Xavier Woods
20. Maryse

54 Mic Drop

1. AJ Styles	9. Enzo Amore
2. Samoa Joe	10. Paige
3. Seth Rollins	11. Dolph Ziggler
4. Chris Jericho	12. The Rock
5. Dean Ambrose	13. Enzo Amore
6. Charlotte	14. Cesaro
7. Roman Reigns	15. Bray Wyatt
8. New Day	

56 SPOT THE DIFFERENCE

58 The Road to *Wrestlemania*

1. John Cena ⟶ Roman Reigns
2. Dean Ambrose ⟶ Undertaker
3. Bray Wyatt ⟶ The Rock
4. Sami Zayn ⟶ Kevin Owens

60 Superstar Spirit Animals

Honey Badger: **DEAN AMBROSE**
Black Panther: **ROMAN REIGNS**
Lion: **TRIPLE H**
Wolf: **BARON CORBIN**
Viper: **RANDY ORTON**
Buzzard: **BRAY WYATT**
Bull: **THE ROCK**
Peacock: **THE MIZ**
Alien: **STARDUST**